2016

W

MW00627682

Best Days

My BEST DAY II

A collection of best day remembrances of celebrities
and other prominent Americans

H- 949-645-810 9

MARK KEYS

Always
Mark Keys

M
C
C
O
O
L

K
E
Y
S

PRESS

McCool Keys Press
5308 Neptune
Newport Beach, CA 92663

Individual Sales, This book is available through most bookstores or
can be ordered directly from McCool Keys Press at the address above.

Quantity Sales. Special discounts are available on quantity purchas-
es by corporations, associations, and others. For details, contact the
"Special Sales Department" at the publisher's address above.

Printed in the United States of America.

Library of Congress Cataloging-in-Publication Data is available
from the publisher.

ISBN 978-0-9897878-5-7

Cover Design Concept by Mark Keys & Kendall Roderick

Cover design and text design by Kendall Roderick (RMind-Design.com)

The text for this book is set in Century

Dedication

For Mom and Don, Dad and Ellen, Laurie, Page, and Megan

For all my other family members and friends who have supported me throughout my recent years of rehabilitation and while preparing this book.

For Danny and Shelia Rogers, Dr. Eberhart and staff, Dr. Gerkin, Dr. Gordon, Dr. Carlson, Dr. Fee, Dr. Cailloutte, Dr. Kimberly Safman, Dr. Lakshmi S Shukla, Dr. Joel R Sheiner, Dr. Robinson, Dr. Stringer, Lem Barney, Start Physical Therapy, Karen Davidson, Karen Martin, Bill Sharman, Ron Lamberton, Rick John, Fred Howser, Steve Foley, Mark & Leslie Louvier, Frank & Glenell, Jerry & Diane Tagami, Ken McLain, Bill Wakeman, Arnold Mendoza, Fay Ireland, Mike Kelly, Hal & Renee Holleman, Craig & Gigi Lyons, Janet Curci Walsh, John Wooden, Mike Wilsey & Family, Rev. Jim Birchfield, Vern Fansler, Joe Rogers, The Helfrich Family.

In memory of Dr. Charles Bellitti, Tyler Mimm, Vincent Arranaga, Lou Rawls, Bill Walsh, James Callahan, Hal and Renee, and Paul Gleeson.

FORWARD:

It is with great joy, pleasure and honor to have been asked to write the foreword to Mark Keys' latest book My Best Day. Mark is my friend, a great brother in Christ, and a truly compelling and inspiring writer and author.

Being a believer and an ordained minister, it's not hard to understand why God places people in our lives. I had the opportunity to meet Mark and his lovely wife Laurie at the Deacon Jones Fundraiser in 2006. It was as if I had known Mark and Laurie all my life. They are a great and loving couple, devoted parents and they love the Lord.

I admire Mark for his courage and tenacity when facing challenges in his life, and always having a never quit/never give up attitude.

My best day was the day I gave my life to Christ, and every day since that day have been my best days. It is a miracle and a blessing every day God wakes us up in our right mind and a reasonable portion of good health·that's a great day. Every day I can pray and spend time with God is one of my best days. God's Love, Grace, and Everlasting Mercy is a Great Day for me no matter what my circumstances or conditions may be. Mark, I commend you on a job well done. Keep inspiring everyone you will meet on this journey of life and for all those who read your books.

— **LEM BARNEY**
Detroit Lions Cornerback,
NFL Hall of Fame Honoree

INTRODUCTION

In May, 1991, I injured my back while working and was placed on permanent disability. Prior to my first back surgery, I had my photo taken with Magic Johnson of the Los Angeles Lakers. Later, Blain Skinner, a friend of mine, was able to get Magic to autograph the snapshot. It made my day.

As a hobby, I began writing to other celebrities asking for autographed photos. Their positive responses amazed me. One weekend while in Palm Springs, California, I met Nat Kipner, and entrepreneur, who suggested I expand my hobby to include famous people from all walks of life. This idea was a godsend. During the next several years, while incapacitated with several more back surgeries and an ankle reconstruction, I collected even more autographs.

One day while out walking, I notice the magnificent beauty of the simple blue sky. Upon returning home, I thought about what a good day it was, despite my back problems. I felt great! Then it struck me: I wondered what all those people I had been receiving autographs from felt was their "best day."

I began writing letters asking that question. Joey Bishop was the first to reply, and that's how it all began. After I collected hundreds of letters, I knew that my collection make an inspirational book. I hope you will agree.

I have had several best days, but to pin it down: When I was liberated from a Japanese POW camp after two and a half years. My best day was freedom.

—LOUIS ZAMPERINI
5000-meter Olympian 1936,
WWI 372nd Bombardment
Squadron, Purple Cross and
Distinguished Flying Cross
Recipient, Author, "Unbroken"

When I sold my book for a thrilling $1,910, and had been promised a first printing of 500 copies. Life had never been so sweet. Second to the birth of my daughter, it was the best day of my life.

—J.K. ROWLING

Author; Harry Potter and Sorcerer's Stone; Harry Potter Series

Everyday is a terrific day. You never know what is going to happen. I have a few BEST days. First, on my eighth birthday I got my dog named Fumble. Another was when I went to Maui and swam by sea turtles. I love spending time with my family or playing at the beach. Volleyball is extra fun with my sister. I love everyday, but some I love more than others, especially if that day is spent with my mom, dad and Megan.

—PAGE KEYS

My Daughter, (at the time of writing this) eleven years old

My best day is when I'm with my wonderful daddy!

—MEGAN KEYS
My daughter, (at the time of writing this) eight years old

Meeting my husband, Mark, was my best day and all of the days to follow. Without him we wouldn't have our wonderful girls, Page and Megan, who bring us both such joy. Life is not always perfect but Mark makes each day brighter.

—LAURIE KEYS

My best day began with driving to Las Vegas listening to Dean Martin singing "Ain't that a Kick in the Head?" on the radio, and then marrying his daughter, Gail, there that night. Now, that was definitely better than a kick in the head.

—**MIKE DOWNEY**
Columnist, Chicago Tribune

When my wife, who is a huge Magic Johnson fan, and I met Magic Johnson at a hospital benefit in Los Angeles. Turns out, Magic Johnson was a big fan of my career with the Raiders and my lite beer commercials. My wife was very impressed. It was a good night.

—BEN DAVIDSON
Football player; Oakland Raiders, Lite Beer All-Star

My "best day" was in September of 1978. It was the day that I gave my Lord Savior Jesus Christ his rightful place in my life. Up to this point in my life I had only known Him as a far-away God—on this day in 1978 I bowed my life to His kingship and I have never had a "better day" in my life. My "best day" was when I declared Jesus as my Lord and Savior—and I started to live in his grace and forgiveness.

—ANDY LOPEZ
Baseball coach, University of Arizona

My best day is yet to come! It may be today or it may be tomorrow. It is that hope that keeps me going.

—SLYVESTER CROOM
Head Football Coach,
Mississippi State

My best day was April 1, 1944. I was commissioned as a second lieutenant with the USMC and I received my Navy Wings of Gold.

—JERRY COLEMAN
Hall of Fame Announcer, San Diego Padres; Ford C. Frick Award Winner

EVERY DAY is my BEST DAY! And I hope your days are the same.

—SIDNEY SHELDON
*Author; Other Side of Midnight
and Naked Face producer;
I Dream of Jeannie*

The best day I ever had occurred in November 1993 when I was inducted into the USA Volleyball Hall of Fame in Holyoke, Massachusetts. It was special because my wife Sue, daughters Tracy and Leslie, son David and son-in-law Stewart shared it with me. My old friend Mike Bright 1964 Olympian was inducted as a player and I became the first active coach ever inducted into the Hall.

It was a perfect "Indian Summer" day and the locals verified that the color of the leaves were the brightest and most beautiful they had seen in many years. We stayed at the historic Hadley House in Springfield and were treated superbly by our local hosts.

Over 700 people attended the banquet, which included many of my old friends from all over the country. There have been many fine days in my life, but because my entire family was there to share this one, it was the best.

—**AL SCATES**
Head Coach, UCLA Volleyball;
nineteen-time NCAA
volleyball title

It is hard to define a "best day" or at least limit it to one. It could be the stormy evening in a cabin in New Mexico with my two sisters while we told stories, laughed and danced the night away. Or it could be when the president of ASU leaned across the table and offered me the position of athletic director. Or...

—LISA LOVE
Athletic Director, ASU

My greatest day! April 13, 1931, my birthday.

—DAN GURNEY
Indy Hall of Fame Racer

My best day was on 15 December 1965. Commanding Gemini Six into the first rendezvous in space. The event led to the successful lunar mission.

—**WALLY SCHIRRA**
Astronaut, Mercury Eight,
Gemini Six, Apollo Seven

I have been struggling to determine just what my "favorite day" would be. I would have to say it would be everyday. Each day that I have the privilege to wake up in the morning and share time with my family and friends, meet the challenges of work, and then rest for the next "favorite day," that's when I know I am blessed.

— DRAYTON McLANE, JR.
Owner/President Houston
Astros, 2005 World Series

As an athlete and coach I have been lucky enough to have many great days. However, none could match the two best days of my life. The day I married my wife, Laura in Napa and the day my daughter Kendall was born.

—JEFF BRINKLEY
*Head football coach, Newport
Harbor High School*

Every day is my best day.

—LLOYD BRIDGES
Actor, Sea Hunt, High Noon

There is no other possibility for my best day than the day Helen Hayes MacArthur and Charles MacArthur decided to adopt me. It made my life what is has been. Without them I have no idea to where I would be. Perhaps in another good place... perhaps not. I am only grateful that I never knew the other option!

—JAMES MACARTHUR
Actor, Hawaii 5-0, Swiss Family Robinson

My best day? Tomorrow.

—**JAMES GREGORY**
Actor, Barney Miller

Any day above ground is a great day to me!

—TERI GARR
Actress, Young Frankenstein,
Tootsie, Mr. Mom, author

It has been said that "God is the giver and the gift." My "best day" is the awareness I have of this gift and my heart will always say "thank you."

—BETSY PALMER

Actress, Marvelous History of
St. Bernard, I've Got a Secret,
Mister Roberts

My "best day" was the day I received your invitation to share a personal thought with response to "What was your best day?" It made me start thinking and realizing what a fortunate person I am. I've had so many "best days" that have meant so much to me. Just thinking through so many of those days and what the memories brought to me, and meant to me, filled my day with happiness and gratitude. What wonderful meaningful memories I had that day about family and friends and work and play. I laughed and cried. It was a day like no other. Thanks for asking. Boy did you make my day.

—ARTHUR HILLER

Director; Love Story, the Out-of-Towners, Plaza Suite

The best day of my life has been "every day," as I have developed the ability to be totally positive about my present and future life. At forty, time to accept negativity in my life.

—BIFF REDDIN
1973 WHA World Cup, LA
Sharks Hockey Coach

My very best days are fifty-nine years ago when I married my wife Joan. We have four charming daughters; Lucy, Lori, Carol and Ellen. Also another best day was when I enrolled at USC in 1946 after being discharged from the US Marine Corps, and played football during 1946 and 1947 seasons, and I finally graduated in 1948.

—WALLY SEMENIUK
USC Football

My best day was the day I was born. I have thoroughly enjoyed my life, so far.

—CONSTANCE TOWERS
Actress, General Hospital,
Horse Soldiers

I've been blessed with so many "best days" that I cannot choose a favorite. Even better—each new morning brings that possibility of yet another "best."

—RICHARD ERDMAN
Actor/Director

My "best day" was Friday the 13th, January 1950. That was the day my first son, Paul Vincent (P.V.), was born. I went on to have four sons and four daughters. I was still a student at Loyola University in Westchester, California, majoring in drama; I was starting on an acting career in motion pictures.

The morning my agent called me and said that I had three interviews for minor roles in three different movies at three different studios. Armed with a pocketful of cigars—I left the bedside of my wife, Marie, and little P.V., at the Culver City Hospital. My first stop was 20th Century Fox Studios and the office of Otto Preminger. The movie was Where the Sidewalk Ends starring Dana Andrews.

The secretary in the outer office suggested I had better not go in to see Mr. Preminger with the cigars, as he hates smokers. I left the cigars on her desk, saw Mr. Preminger and got the part, a one-day "bit."

Next I went to RKO Studios to see Mel Ferrer, the director of Secret Fury. Again I got the part of a doctor in a scene with Claudette Colbert. It was a nice part, I had to learn a new word "electroencephalograph." My next stop was Columbia Studios for a picture, "The Killer that Stalked New York". The small part was mine. Best of all, the three jobs didn't conflict. I was able to do all of them.

What a day—my first son and three movies to help pay for the hospital bill. Today P.V. is 56-years old (I'm 83) and working as a property master in TV and films. He's a good son and is right there when Marie and I need a chore done.

—PAUL PICERNI

Actor, The Killer that Stalked New York, Operation Pacific, The Scalphunters

Each day that I wake up becomes my best!

—MIKE CONNERS
Actor, Mannix, Good Sam

My first recording deal and entering the Rock &
Roll Hall of Fame.

—MARTY BALIN
Musician, Jefferson Airplane

I finally decided that if I had one choice it would be the day I was discharged from the Army in November, 1945. To have gotten through World War II alive and well was a miracle that allowed me to get on with my life that produced so many "best days." That day was symbolic of my incredible good fortune.

—**JACK WHITAKER**
Hall of Fame announcer

I have had so many wonderful days in my life and I can't begin to think of which was the BEST. Maybe when I married my beautiful, fabulous wife, Joanie (37-years ago), maybe when my two handsome sons were born, maybe my first Ed Sullivan show, when I called my mother in Boston and she was so proud. Maybe when Joanie and I stayed with the Sinatra family several times in Rancho Mirage, maybe when I was asked to accompany Tom Jones on his first American tour. Maybe the day that Jimmy Cagney came to my house for the first time and I was so excited that I tried to call everyone from my old gang in Boston but most of them were in jail.

There have been so many memorable days but I think over all when I had an MRI after treatment and weeks of radiation for a tumor under my tongue that was completely gone and that I was healthy... that could have been it.

—NORM CROSBY
Comedian/Actor

My best day was VJ Day... August 1945, the day World War II ended and I, along with 16 million others, came home to the US.

—MARV LEVY
Coach, Vice President and General Manager, Buffalo Bills

My best day was March 5, 1948 when I married Anne Jackson. This coming March will be our 55th anniversary and we're still working..

—ELI WALLACH
Actor, The Good, the Bad and
the Ugly, Magnificent Seven

My best day? Hmm ... wasn't just one. Bunches!
When I got married, when my children were born,
when I got my first roll in a movie ... TOMORROW!

—L. Q. JONES
Actor, Casino, The Sacketts

I have to say that my best day was the opening night of Zoot Suit at Mark Taper Forum in Los Angeles.

—EDWARD JAMES OLMOS
Actor, Miami Vice

I was having one of my best days in Palm Springs attending our friend Barbara Sinatra's fundraiser for her center for abused children, when Mark Keys asked me to send him a description of my "best day."

I gave it a lot of thought and realized that I am lucky to have had so many best days that I am now going to write my own damn book. Like Pearl Bailey said, "If I can't sell it, I'm going to sit down on it, because I ain't giving nothin' away."

So Mark, you go buy my book and I'll buy yours and that way we'll both have another "best day."

—GEORGE SCHLATTER
Writer/Producer, Laugh-In,
American Comedy Awards

Every day I consider a best day. It is too difficult to pick just one. I just thank God for all my blessings.

—JULIA MEADE
Actress, Pillow Talk

Any day I can play jazz on the radio is my best day.

—CHUCK NILES
*Radio Announcer; Hollywood
Walk of Fame*

45

My best day was September 21, 1958 when I married Toby. Except I never realized it was until she passed away on June 21, 2001. It was 43 years of best days. My three boys understand this and love me even though they know they're in second place.

—JED ALLAN
Actor, Days of our Lives,
Santa Barbara

I was in the Navy in World War II after two years in the South Pacific when our ship sailed under the Golden Gate Bridge in San Francisco—Officers and crew broke down and cried. That was my best day...

—LARRY STORCH
Actor, F Troop, Sex and the Single Girl, The Great Race

After much reflection, the obvious banner days of four healthy children brought into this world ... I feel the best day was when film icon Robert Redford invited me to play legendary Twenty-One TV host, Jack Berry, in his acclaimed film, Quiz Show. What made it so special was he did that with just a look into my eyes, artist to artist, with an audition—and he knew I could do it. It remains a high point in my filmography.

—**CHRIS McDONALD**
Actor, Quiz Show, Spy Kids,
Happy Gilmore

When I was 11-years old and the public school music system in Rochester, New York, handed me an oboe I never heard of before, and that was the beginning of my career.

—MITCH MILLER
Grammy Award Winner; Musician; The Mitch Miller Show

My best day was when I was hired for "Days" (Days of Our Lives) and B&B (The Bold and the Beautiful).

— JOSEPH MASCOLO
Actor, Days of Our Lives, Bold and the Beautiful

The best days of my life (two) were when I gave birth to my children.

—BLYTHE DANNER
Actress, Huff, Westworld

I've had many best days, but I think the day of my marriage heads the pack.

—HORTON FOOTE
*Screenwriter, To Kill a Mocking-
bird, Trip to Bountiful*

It is very difficult to pinpoint a "best day" in my life I've had many good and very good days for which I am most thankful. Probably the three best days were when each of my three sons was born. I'm very proud of them all.

—**WARREN STEVENS**
Actor, Twilight Zone,
Falcon Crest

My "best day" hasn't arrived yet! But I've had a lot of "better days."

—JAMIE FARR
Actor, With Six You Get Eggrolls, M*A*S*H

Today! Tonight I found that I had checked every item on my "to do" list, and I'll go to sleep knowing that I gave this day my very best "shot," my very best effort—a day couldn't be any better than that!

—ROGER WILLIAMS
Grammy award winning pianist

The day I met my wife, Patricia!

—RICHARD HERD
Actor, Home Alone, Seinfeld

Wow! As the years encroach upon my memories, I think of all the loving, sharing and laughing in a sweeping continuum so that one day does not stick out as better than many others ...

My children's births, my happy youthful exuberance and prolonged periods without pain are among those I enjoyed immensely... Oh yes, there was another... the day Nixon died. Mean as that sounds, it was much meaner to be on his enemies list.

—AVERY SCHREIBER
Comedian, My Mother the car,
Robin Hood:Men in Tights

We live by hope for tomorrow. So I guess my best day is yet to come. It's something to always look forward to— "Look-look-look to the rainbow."

—NORMAN JEWISON
Award-winning director,
Cincinnati Kid

The day I was born (November 20, 1908!) on my father's birthday.

—**ALISTAIR COOKE**
Actor/Narrator/Broadcaster
Masterpiece Theatre, Three
Faces of Eve

I've had many best days in my life—the best two days were on September 20, 1952 when I married Dr. Leo Fred. He was a wonderful husband. We had 42 joyous years together—he passed away several years ago—I miss him every day.

The other best day was when I gave birth to my lovely daughter Mary Elizabeth Ann on June 25, 1954. She is the joy of my life and has given me two wonderful grandchildren, Noah and Maggie.

—AUDREY TOTTER
Actress, Carpetbaggers, The Postman Always Rings Twice

I did not have just one "best day." All four days when my four children were born would equally be my "best days."

—ROBERT BALLARD, PhD
Discovered the Titanic

I just cannot answer your question. My lifetime honestly gives me a best day everyday, nearly every week.

—BING RUSSELL
Actor, Gunfight at the O.K. Corral, Magnificent Seven

My best day is every day, cause I'm in charge—I plan it—I fix it—I enjoy it always.

—RIP TORN
Comedian, actor, Crosscreek,
Men in Black

Best Days:

1) January 27, 1981 I met my wife, Jane Powell.

2) May 21, 1988 when we got married.

—DICKIE MOORE
*Actor, Our Gang, Heaven Can
Wait, Oliver Twist*

I have too many "best days" to pick out any one day.

—BETTY GARRETT
Actress, On the Town

I was "in the zone" so to speak when I took 15 shots and made 14—all 12 fouls and scored 40 points in a college game while playing for C. W. Post College on Long Island.

Great are the days with the birth of my five kids and meeting the "love of my life," Marchell Williams, in a cemetery in Westwood in front of Dean Martin's resting place. It is a great journey for both of us. Another great day was having Alfred Hitchcock say how much he wanted me for a film. Everyday is a big sandwich—remember to take a big bite out of it and enjoy the experience of life.

—ED LAUTER
Actor, The Longest
Yard, Seabiscuit

I got goose bumps peering through the small triangular window onto the craggy surface of the moon. The Lunar Module's descent was perfect. nearly hyperventilating with excitement, I pushed off the last rung of the ladder and dropping gently onto the powdery—wait a minute—that wasn't me…that was an astronaut, you know, uh, what's his name…oh well. Hey, I'll bet that was his best day though.

—**BRYAN CRANSTON**
Actor, Malcolm in the Middle,
Saving Private Ryan,
Breaking Bad

It had to have been when my mother, Jennie Nelson and my father, Billie Nelson put me, my grandmother and a few others on a train to New York City, New York from Henderson, North Carolina. Without that move, there would be no Ben E. King.

—BEN E. KING
Singer, "Stand by Me"

EVERYDAY!

—GARY MORTON
Actor/Producer

When I met my wife.

—KARL MALDEN
Actor, Streets of San Francisco,
Street Car Named Desire

When I think of one best day there is absolutely no way I can come up with just one. However, I think my best days have been those when I have had some sort of adversity or challenge to overcome. When things are going well it is easy to jump into the current and ride it out. I prefer days that have challenges and even adversity. Adversity and challenges are what makes us stronger and in my opinion they are often blessings in disguise. Finding positive answers to negative situations truly makes each and every day a great one.

—ANDY LANDERS
University of Georgia women's Basketball Coach

My best day was when my son Christopher was born, May 30, 1980. I was lucky enough to be there with my wife, Peggy and support her through the delivery. It was not only an amazing physical event, but to have a healthy and beautiful son; I can't describe the feeling of pride and excitement. To this day that pride and excitement continues to grow along with the same feeling about our daughter Kathleen.

—CRAIG HARTSBURG
Anaheim Ducks NHL
Hockey Coach

June 27, 1964 was my best day. I married my high school sweetheart, Pam White. Thirty-five years, three children and four grandchildren later I realize what a special day it was. I also realize it was my luckiest day!

—DAN REEVES
NFL Player Dallas Cowboys;
Atlanta Falcons and Denver
Bronco Football Coach

I think my husband, Edward, would have answered this way: "My best day was when I was released from the agony of being alive the last days."

—EDWARD DMYTRYK

As told by his wife, Jean, director, Caine Mutiny, Young Lions

Today is my best day! I have all of the yester-
days to remember and all the tomorrows to look
forward to.

—LLOYD BOCHNER
Actor, Dynasty, Twilight Zone

The day I was born.

—EDDIE ALBERT
*Actor, Green Acres, The
Longest Yard*

My "best day" was the last day of filming in Death Valley on "Three Godfathers" in July, 1948. The reason it was my best day was because John Ford was very, very hard on me all through the filming of "Three Godfathers".

—HARRY CAREY JR.
Actor, Tombstone, The Searchers

My "best day" is today and my next "best day" is tomorrow and every day is my "best day."

—LARRY HAGMAN
*Actor, Dallas, I Dream
of Jeannie*

M_y best day was January 21, 1981 when I saw my best friend Ronald Reagan sworn in as President of the United States in Washington. He appointed me to his advisory board with offices in the OEB at the White House.

Another "best day" was the first time I saw the title on the screen "Produced by A. C. Lyles." My career at Paramount had advanced from office boy for Adolph Zucker, founder of Paramount to producer.

Another best day was when I celebrated my 80th birthday and at the same time my 70th anniversary with Paramount. It's a short resume, "1928-2000: Paramount."

—**A. C. LYLES**
Producer, Young and the Brave,
Red Tomahawk

The best day is always today.

—DICK MARTIN

Actor/Comedian/Director, Rowan & Martins Laugh-in

Best Day:

Getting married.

First child born.

Second child born.

—DENY JACOBSEN
Vice Principal, Horace Ensign
Junior High

I have thought about my "best day" and have concluded that each day God gives me is my "best day."

—WILLARD SCOTT
NBC weatherman

I've had a lot of good ones, a number of bad ones, and a bunch in between. It is also true that I look to my days right now and in the future for some degree of joy and satisfaction. I guess I dwell much on the past.

—LEN LESSER
Actor, Seinfeld, "Uncle Leo",
The Outlas Josey Wales

My best day is always the next day.

— ANDREW V. McLAGLEN
Director, Chisum, McLintock!

I have been very fortunate to have so many wonderful days from which to choose. I would have to say that the most special days for me would have to be the days my three children, Kara, Teddy and Patrick were born. Family is very important to me and my children have always been a source of joy for me.

Among the other days in my life that I would consider to be the most special would be the day John Kennedy was elected President of the United States. His inauguration was also a day of great pride for my family and me.

My first election to the Senate in 1962 was a very special day for me, as was the day of my re-election in 1995. It is always a distinct honor to be elected to serve the people of Massachusetts.

I am grateful to have memories of so many wonderful days and I hope that sharing them with you will help you with your project.

—SENATOR EDWARD
M. KENNEDY

Any day in which I receive letters from fans, re-minding me that all my years of hard work mak-ing quality entertainment did make a difference, and my efforts were worthwhile and appreciated by good people.

—DAVID DORTORT

Creator and Producer, Bonanza,
High Chaparral

Every day is my best day and each day gets better and better. What you think is the reason for having great days. The two most memorable "best days" were:

June 22, 1976 when my daughter, Taylor Van was born and her dad, Bobby Van was announcing the birth on his morning show on NBC and February 10, 1986 when my son, Mick Levoff was born. I don't think it gets better than that.

—ELAINE JOYCE
Actress, Love Boat, Beverly Hills 90210

Every day is my best day!

—JERRY MATHERS
Actor, Leave it to Beaver

The day I won the Emmy Award. It topped off my career, now life is a pleasure.

—ALEX ROCCO
Actor, Godfather Trilogy,
Get Shorty, The Famous Teddy Z

I thank the Lord there have been so many best days... The day I married; the day each of my four children were born; the day I signed to star at the Paramount Theatre on Broadway; the day I signed for my first TV show; the day I signed for my first movie; the day I signed for my first Broadway musical/comedy; and so many more. I guess the answer is October 4th, 19_... the day I was born.

—JAN MURRAY
Actor/Comedian, Thunder Alley

The days of my childhood were for the most marvelous; my teen years were exciting and different than most young men my age; my coming home safe from the war; my first child; my first important job; my second child; my first break in nightclub; my third child; my first break in a Broadway play; my fourth child; my first break in TV; the births of my grandchildren; meeting my present wife; the wonderful moments we've spent together … maybe my best day lies ahead—I doubt if these can be topped but I'll look forward to it anyway!

I envy no one. I've had an incredible life—my best day? How could I possibly measure it?

—PETER MARSHALL
Actor/Singer, TV host,
Hollywood Squares

My best day was the summer of '63. Living in our first home which had a half acre of hillside. My wife had gone to the obstetrician being with our soon to be firstborn. I was clearing brush on the slope with a big guy from North Carolina and Howard, his wino helper. All of a sudden I see our car coming up the water tank road which bottomed our property. I became fearful that something had gone wrong at the doctors. Then I relaxed knowing she wouldn't be driving like a bat out of hell if she weren't in a good mood. She got out of the car and imperiously ordered me to come down the slope to her. I snarled, "What for?" and she demanded my descent. Halfway down I stopped, looked at her and said "Really?" and she smiled and nodded yes. I leaped for joy and guessed she'd found out we were having twins. What a nice day, I shouted to the Carolinian, "Bill, she's having twins!" and he congratulated me. Then not wanting to slight the wino I said, "Howard, she's having twins" and he responded, "Yeah, I'm a twin, I clutched my heart and fought to keep from asking, "What does your brother do?"

—**ED ASNER**
Actor, Mary Tyler Moore Show,
Lou Grant

My best day was being on M*A*S*H*.

—WAYNE ROGERS
*Actor, M*A*S*H*, House Calls*

While we all hope our "best day" has not yet come, so I assume you mean "so far." Very well:

My first lovemaking.

My first time in love.

My first play.

The day I knew I would be a play writer.

—EDWARD ALBEE
Playwright, Who's Afraid of
Virginia Wolf, honoree,
Kennedy Center Honors

One of my best days was meeting my idol, Frank Sinatra and being his protégée.

—TRINI LOPEZ
Singer/Actor; The Dirty Dozen

My best days are those when I do not think of myself.

—NANCY OLSON
*Actress, The Absent Minded
Professor, Sunset Boulevard*

There is no way I could pick a "best" or a "worst." I have been blessed with so may great days and events that each, although different, is special. And none of them would mean as much if not contrasted with some dismal dark days. Often people ask me to choose a favorite role, or picture and my usual flip answer is, "the next one."

In the same light I have been asked WHO IN-SPIRED ME MOST and again there are so many equal choices. I have decided that, for me, life is a composite and I couldn't appreciate something today if I hadn't experienced something earlier to give it perspective. Nor could a joy today be as great were it not contrasted with a soul-shaking sorrow.

—DABBS GREER
Actor, Rockford Files, Cannon,
The Green Mile

My best day? Easy! December 25, 2005. The birth of Christ and the day I found out my wife, Sam, was pregnant with our first child.

—KEVIN SORBO
Actor, Hercules

What an order this is... my best day! Only one per customer? I have been married for 45 years, I have two children and four wonderful grand-children--roughly five careers, that means a lot of great days, some family-oriented, some career-related, some deeply personal. I guess I would have to say August 8, 1956—the day my daughter, Pamela was born—our first child. She was fine. Jill, my wife, was fine, and all I had to do was relish the moment and seek new meaning for the word love. There is something amazing about a first child—we prove so much about ourselves on that day. So many fears are gone for good, on that day. I supposed it is mundane—but that would be my day—with a subset of July 20, 1959 when our second child, Clay, was born.

—ROGER CARAS
Actor, 2001 Space Odyssey

I am guessing that you have in mind a best day other than my marriage day in 1947 or the birth days of our four children, right?

All of those days stand alone. In another category, my best day was July 11, 1945. After two years of flight training, I made the mandatory number of landings aboard the USS Wolverine to qualify as a Navy Carrier Pilot, flying the "Wildcat" fighter plane designated FM-2... made by Grumman. Going out the gate to celebrate that evening, Johnny Mercer's "On the Atchison, Topeka & the Santa Fe" record was playing on the PX. I can still feel the joy of my "best day."

—**CHUCK CECIL**
Radio Announcer

When I met Frank.

—BARBARA SINATRA
Philanthropist

My best day? Today!

—**BETTY WHITE**
*Actress, Golden Girls, Mary
Tyler Moore Show*

Aside from my three Children being born ... the day World War II ended. I was in Iwo Jima and hadn't seen my wife for sixteen months.

—CARL REINER
Actor/Writer; The Dick Van Dyke Show, author

The day I auditioned for the movie, From Here to Eternity. My career was at an all-time low and I had to pull strings to get an audition. I knew I was born to play Maggio. I did the "bar scene" and improvised by picking up olives to use as dice to roll "snake eyes" to impress the director. I got the role and went on to win an Oscar for Best Supporting Actor as Maggio.

—**FRANK SINATRA**
As told by Tom Dreesen, Actor/
Singer; Suddenly, Man with the
Golden Arm

My best day is truly everyday!! May love and romance be in your life always,

—TOVA BORGNINE
Beauty products, wife of
Ernest Borgnine

My best days were when I married my wife and when each one of my three children were born.

—LALO SCHIFRIN
Composer, "Mission Impossible"

My best day is being with family and friends.

—MAUREEN McCORMICK
Actress/Singer; Brady Bunch

My best day was January 14, 1939. That was the lucky day when I married Ruth Barth. We have been happily married now for 57 years and hope to stay healthy and happy for many more.

—PAUL HENNING
Producer, Petticoat Junction,
Green Acres, Beverly Hillbillies

This is the best day to give all Glory to God—
Father, Son and Holy Spirit.

—LANE BRODY
Country Western Singer

In a life filled with several "special days" in so many different facets of my life, I suppose that choosing that "one special day" really depends on your audience. What is it they can understand? Which of several tales shall I tell/ There are all the standard "special days" like the birth days of my children, marriage to my current wife, that significant day when I realized I was okay with never having another drink...and there are the professional moments when my work actually paid off (though seldom with hard dollars).

Then, too, there are moments that for a person who has been in the public eye for more than 40 years, are almost expected...such as being recognized for the first time by a stranger, the feeling of hitting #1 on the record charts, or a live performance that brought an audience to its feet... but so much of that seems to be bragging and is seldom seen for what it is...a moment in time in a performer's life and nothing more. So I choose to tell you about doing the impossible. That is something everyone understands.

—**PAUL PETERSEN**
Actor/Singer, The Donna Reed Show; Minor Consideration- kid actors- past and present; founder/president

My best day in sports; in 1970 when we beat Anaheim on our way to the first Sunset League Football Championship Newport harbor Football had in 28 years. That season was epic!

My best two days were the days Eric and Shea were born (son and daughter). That gave true meaning to my life as a parent and father. There are too many best days in my life as these are but a few. Seeing our children mature and improve has been a great part of my life, enjoying my many friendships and finding my life partner in Terri.

—TONY HORVATH
Newport Harbor football player

My best day is every day. I am blessed by just waking up.

—ELAINE STRITCH
Actress, My Sister Eileen, Trails of O'Brien

Everyday I'm alive is my "best day." I'm now 71 so I've had a lot of best days.

—JOHN FIELDER
Actor, Bob Newhart Show, voice of Piglet

Best days are abundant when we have a positive outlook. Some of the many best days are:

The birth of my children.

The blessing of my marriage to Christopher, later to Doug.

That time in the ice cave.

Each day that I awake with the blessings of the Great Spirits of the universe.

—LINDA DAY GEORGE
Actress, Mission Impossible,
Rich Man, Poor Man

Looking back on my life, filled with very many good days—to choose one I could honestly call the "best" is totally impossible. I look forward to the rest of my life with the same sort of impartiality— each day is a wonder unto itself.

—KIM HUNTER
Actress, Planet of the Apes,
Streetcar named Desire

The best day I ever had was my first appearance at Carnegie Hall in 1964. It was a thrill I will never forget.

As far as personally, it was the day my son was born, and four years later when my daughter was born. Of course getting married was also a great day in my life.

—JERRY VALE
Singer

Giving birth to my two children, they are 20-years apart and I never thought I could have my daughter. She now has two babies so those days are also very special.

—GWEN VERDON
Actress/Dancer, Damn Yankees,
Magnum PI

The first response that comes to mind when you ask me about my best day is the morning I got to meet and interview Katharine Hepburn at her brownstone apartment in New York City. She couldn't have been more forthcoming and we seemed to hit it off right away. I had seen a mutual friend a few days earlier so that was my icebreaker and it seemed to work. While the crew was setting up our cameras, we chatted, and when we moved into position to do the "official" interview, we simply kept it up. She's a great interview because she is so direct and opinionated. It doesn't hurt that she leads a fascinating life. When our allotted time was over, I didn't want to leave…and in fact, I didn't, until every bit of equipment was packed up and there was no way to linger another minute. I'll never forget that day.

—LEONARD MALTIN
*Movie Critic, Entertainment
Tonight, author*

Having all my sons together when the youngest one got married. One even flew in from London first for the event, then flew right out to South America on business.

—ELINOR DONAHUE
Actress, Andy Griffith Show,
Father Knows Best

My best day was VE Day in 1945. To see the jubilation all around me as a young fella, knowing that so many loved ones would be coming home after the long ordeal both over there and at home.

—PAUL GLEASON
Actor, Trading Places,
Breakfast Club

October 6, 1993--I was shooting Picket Fences at 20th Century Fox (it's always a good day when an actor is working). But it turned into my best day when Peggy and I met at the commissary—we wed the following May—my Irish Colleen has made my life complete.

—JAMES CALLAHAN
Actor, M*A*S*H*, Charles in Charge

Every morning is the best day of my life. At 82 years of age each day is a gift and with it goes the obligation to be thankful for it and to use it fully, wisely and well, both for enrichment of my life but also for those whose lives I will touch as my best days go by.

—EARL HAMNER
Creator/Narrator,
Waltons, author

My best day is always today, the "now." No use brooding over the past or fantasizing over the future. The only time we really have is "now." It's our only chance to do our best and to be our best.

—JOANNA BARNES
Actress, Parent Trap

My best day is many days. I treasure the days of my youth when my wonderful parents raised my two sisters and me. I cannot forget the day I first saw my wife, Shelley, who was a coed at the University of Cincinnati, and later when we married. Certainly, the birthdays of our three children were days I consider as best days.

In almost 20 years of coaching, my best days were the days that I personally touched the lives of others and made a difference. Today is my best day as I write this letter to you in hopes that I too can make this your best day.

—URBAN MEYER
Head Football Coach,
University of Florida

"Each day God grants us is better than the day before." Go Bucks!

—JIM TRESSEL
Head Football Coach,
Ohio State

My best day is receiving a thoughtful letter from you (Mark). Your letter brought me joy. Your desire to bring happiness to others is indeed my "best day." Hope I spread a little joy on your day.

—SONNY LUBICK
Montana State and Colorado
College Football Coach

I have been very blessed in my life to have a lot of great days but without a doubt the day my twin daughters, (Victoria and Alexis) were born, July 2, 1996 is the greatest day of all. My wife, Annemarie, was having labor pains in the evening. So we went to the hospital and they hooked her up to the monitors. When our doctor arrived he said the babies weren't coming now but they could come anytime the next couple of days. As I was to travel to Chicago July 4th, and the girls were going to be taken C-section, my wife said she would be mortified if they were born while I was gone. I would have been mortified too. The doctor said the girls were healthy and it had been 36 weeks so we decided to do it right then.

—COREY BLACK
Horse Jockey

My first four best days have been, of course, my four great progency gang: Michael, Timothy, Lindsey and Kelly! My fifth best day was the day I was notified that I had been nominated for an Emmy Award (one of six nominees), for best actor in a comedy series. I didn't win, but I got a "nommy."

—BILL ERWIN
Actor; Dennis the Menace, Man
from Del Rio, Home Alone

There have been so many "best days" for Alvy that it is very hard to pick just one. I've talked it over with my son, Barry, and my daughter, Alyson, and they felt the following would be of most interest:.

Alvy was raised in southern Indiana, so he was quite honored to be invited as a celebrity guest to the INDY 500 race. (I can't remember the year, but my son is researching it as he and his family joined us that weekend because they were living in Indiana at that time.)

Alvy was appearing in Green Acres as Hank Kimball (the county agent) at the time. He was in the parade the day before the race, with all the race car drivers, through downtown Indianapolis...but the big thrill was the next day. Just before the start of the race they drove us around the track in an open convertible. To hear that crowd of thousands calling his name and cheering was a moment I'll never forget. The electricity in the air was unbelievable. The fans were so keyed up for the big race.

— CAROLYN MOORE
Widow and on behalf of Alvy
Moore, Actor; Green Acres

My best day was October 7, 1998. That was the day my daughter Grace Eva was born. We were playing the Cleveland Indians in game two of the American League Championship series. I was at the hospital with my wife and learned that the Yankees had lost the game. However, as any parent will tell you, it was my "best day" ever.

—BRIAN CASHMAN
General Manager, New York Yankees

There was a program in Hollywood which judged all the up and coming new records called "Is it a hit or a miss?" I can't remember the year but it was about the release of my first record. It was called "Black Magic" and it was my first release on Capitol. They had guest panelists judging the records and everyone at Capitol was listening on the air to see these four panelists who were judging Freddie Slack's orchestra and the vocals by Margaret Whiting. I was sitting on the edge of my bed at home chewing my nails and had finished my left hand when the first two people judged it a hit and 100 percent. I started to work on my second hand and then stopped when the third and forth panelists judged it a hit and 100 percent. Then people called me from all over the city saying "congratulations, you've got a hit," and I said to myself, Congratulations Margaret, you have no nails left." Believe it or not that was the first thing that I had done in my professional career and to get four 100 percents was the best thing that happened to me.

—MARGARET WHITING
Professional Singer

Life is a best day.

—JANE ALEXANDER
Actress, Miracle on 34th Street

My best day was October 22, 1975. The day my daughter was born! What a life changing and enriching day!

—KIM STANLEY

Actress, Séance on a Wet Afternoon

I think my best day was when I took all the Lennon Sisters on a date—then I met my wife!

—GARY OWNES

Professional radio personality,
Rowan & Martin's Laugh-in,
Author "How to make a million
dollars with your voice or lose
your tonsils"

My best day was when I submitted my life to the Lord at a young age. Our relationship has grown to great heights, all because I said yes to Jesus, who is my best friend. I spend just about all of my days with Him, the rest of the time I'm doing His work, what a friend I have in Jesus.

—LEM BARNEY
Hall of Fame Professional Football Player, Detroit Lions

I am very glad to have you both as my fans, now as far as my best day, I have had many great days. number one was when I was told my record was a hit, another was when I met my husband, another was when I met Michael Landon and he asked me if I wanted to come on Little House on the Prairie and of course when my child was a boy, because that was what my husband wanted.

—KETTY LESTER
Actress/Singer, Little House of the Prairie

I'm going to take the liberty to split your request into two answers:

My best day is yet to come because I look forward to the challenge of upcoming projects, always with the knowledge that there are solutions for everything. I look on tomorrow as the "best day" opportunity.

Regarding past experiences--particularly related to sports:

My best day from the past was January 12, 1970 the day after the Chiefs had won Super Bowl IV.

It specifically relates to the Victory Parade and celebration through the downtown area and on to the Liberty memorial in Kansas City. Thousands of fans had congregated to be part of the event. The Chiefs winning the game the day before was fun, but seeing the reactions of the fans was the icing on the cake for my "best day."

—LAMAR HUNT
AFL founder, Kansas City
Chiefs Owner

In 1980 I was shot three times in New York by a deranged attendant at a parking lot. I survived and that was a pretty good day. But, On September 17, 1989 I fell from a ladder (12-feet high) broke my neck in six places C1-2-4-5-C7 and T1; entered the hospital as a quadriplegic. They said I'd never walk again. On November 17, 1989 I walked out of the hospital wearing a halo and using two Canadian crutches—but I did walk out, very slowly—but I walked out! That was my best day.

—ART METRANO
Actor; Love Me, Love Me Not,
Moving' On, Tim Conway
Comedy Hour

Right after I turned six I had become so good at walking that my mom and dad put my walker in the attic forever, that was my best day.

—HOPE BRADBURY
age 6

My best day was the day I caught a stingray off of the dock at my papa's house.

—LUKE BRADBURY
age 9

As a cast member in Peter Pan my best day was when I flew across a stage while performing for my school, friends, and family.

—SARA BRADBURY
age 11

My best day was on my birthday when all of my friends and family, Papa too, were sitting around the table to sing "Happy Birthday" to me and have cake with me. I was four that day. Also, when Mark gave me a dollar to buy an ice cream cone.

—JANE MARGARET BRADBURY
age 5

After much thought, I am certain that my best day was the day I chose to embrace the challenges and gifts in each and every day. When Hope was diagnosed with Tuberous Sclerosis I thought it was the end of the world. I had the rest of my life planned out and it did not include a disabled child. God had thrown me a curve ball that I did not have a bat big enough for. Eventually I realized that God had specifically chosen me, my husband, and my family; I was not in charge. The burden had been lifted, I was not cursed but blessed.

—LARA BRADBURY
Mom of Hope, Luke, Sara and Jane

Athletically my "best day" would be too hard to narrow down to just one day. There is no one game, no one particular award, no one practice or one lesson learned on the basketball or volleyball court that could be considered my "best day." To better justify my "best day" would be through the collection of the times and relationships I have experienced throughout my involvement in sports. My "best day" was every game and every practice that I was healthy building those relationships with my teammates and siblings. Those experiences and relationships have taught me many life lessons that are way more important than any one game or award. A special game lasts only a limited amount of time, but the lessons I have learned through sports will be carried on for a lifetime. Of every award I received, of every game we won, nothing can compare to those experiences and relationships I have created through my athletic endeavors. With that said, because of sports, my "best day" is every day through the interaction with my family and friends.

—GREG PERRINE
NHHS basketball and
volleyball player

I thought of several "best day" and each of them was indeed a best day; our wedding, the birth of our first child, my first byline in Life, receiving the first copy of my first book, our 50th wedding anniversary celebration with 6 children, 4 spouses and 12 grandchildren present.

Yet what I think of as my best day looked on the face of it like my worst day. It was late on a sleeting March afternoon in 1945 just west of the Rhine in Germany when I caught a piece of shrapnel in my right hip from a mortar burst.

We had been pinned down but now the enemy was pulling back and the rest of the company was taking off forward. I realized I couldn't move my right leg. My sergeant knelt beside me and said, "yeah, they got you," and dumped some sulfa powder in the wound and put a compress on it. "The medics will be along," he promised and ran off to join the advance.

I estimated it was about four hours before the medics found us. It was too dark to see my match--to see anything. The medics zeroed in on the shouts of the wounded lying elsewhere on the field on the outskirts of the village. But at last I was carried to a Jeep with racks for stretchers and we drove off toward a field hospital in Aachen.

Looking back, I am always surprised that I wasn't really scared. It was almost an out-of-body experience and I seemed to be watching myself lying in the freezing rain. What I felt then, and still, was a fierce pride. I was far from being a warrior, a bespectacled 18-year old so thin I joked I could hide by turning sideways. But I had served, been under fire for three months, been shot at and now had been wounded. I couldn't tell then how bad my wound was (I was back on duty by late summer), but I could tell my grandchildren, if I ever had any, that I had been a combat infantryman in the last good war.

—**CHARLES CHAMPLINN**
Retired columnist,
Los Angeles Times

You would think asking someone to share their "best day" would be a simple thing. Although several thoughts/pictures ran through my mind, I truly feel I have had a lot of "best days." I am very even tempered (almost to a fault) and I don't get too high or too low. I think this allows me to have or enjoy great days or moments because I actually get a lot of joy out of the little things in life. Even a "down day" can provide a "best moment" so I just enjoy them as they come day by day. Hook 'em!

—**CONNIE CLARK**
Basketball Coach, Texas Longhorns

My best day?...When I was 14 and discovered acting. Every day has been a best day ever since.

—GENA ROWLANDS
Actress, Lonely are the Brave

My best day athletically would have to be winning game seven of the 2002 World Series and getting to hold the World Series Trophy!

—TIM SALMON
Baseball Player, Angels

The Ali Fights

—KEN NORTON
Professional Heavyweight Boxer,
1975 Heavyweight title

Choosing my best USC day is not an easy task. I experienced great days in and around USC as a coach's kid; as a player, a fan, and now as an administrator. I saw the 1962 National Championship; Fertig to Sherman in 1964; played on the greatest team ever in 1972; and caught two touchdown passes during the 1974 SC 55 – 24 win against Notre Dame. But, my best day came in my last game and on my last play as a Trojan. On January 1st, 1975 I caught a 38 yard touchdown pass from my best friend, Pat Haden, with 2:03 remaining in the game and after the 2-point conversion we won the game 18-17 over Ohio State. As a result we won the National Championship and my best friend and I were named Co-Rose Bowl MVP's. It doesn't get a lot better than that!

—**JK McKay Jr.**
USC Wide Receiver
1974

My Best Day was the Rose Bowl, 1975. It was my last game and I was a Senior. I thought it was my last game as a player, due to being accepted at Oxford as a Rhodes Scholar. While at USC, I was blessed to play in 3 Rose Bowl Games. In the final Rose Bowl Game, we were playing Ohio State for the National Championship. Back then, the game was a big deal: the Pac 8 vs. Big 8. I threw a winning touchdown to my best pal, J.K. McKay, Jr. and then went for a two-point conversion, to Shelton Diggs for the win. The result was USC being National Champions. Final score: 18-17.

—PAT HADEN
USC Quarterback, 1975, USC Athletic Director.

My greatest moment was when a Special Olympian turned around and gave me a kiss after her event.

—**ROGER "Coach" VAN PELT**
Special Olympics

About the Author:

Mark Keys is a Southern California native, residing in Costa Mesa with his wife Laurie, daughters, Page and Megan, their dog, Fumble, and two cats, Lucy and Ethel. Mark loves that his mom still lives at the beach in Newport in the house he grew up in, and he spends a lot of time there with her & the girls and walking the beach. He played basketball growing up, in High School, and beyond as well as body surfed until he injured his back. Mark is an avid reader, enjoys watching classic movies & westerns, collecting film and sports memorabilia, walking and listening to Jazz, Motown & Rat Pack music, and hanging out with friends. He also loves to travel and going to sporting events & college practices, when health permits. In spite of thousands of hours of physical therapy and his numerous surgeries, including 6 back, 9 ankle, 9 knee, and 2 shoulder surgeries, he also experienced shingles, pneumonia, MRSA Staph infection, prostate infection, concussions, he has no immune system and fights continuous headaches and other health issues every day. But, through all of this, he keeps a positive attitude and outlook to make each day, his best day.

25332834R00088

Made in the USA
San Bernardino, CA
27 October 2015